YOU CHOOSE

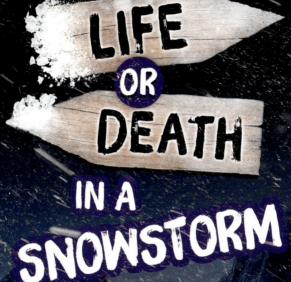

LIFE OR DEATH
IN A SNOWSTORM

AN INTERACTIVE SURVIVAL ADVENTURE

BY JESSICA GUNDERSON

CAPSTONE PRESS
a capstone imprint

Published by Capstone Press, an imprint of Capstone
1710 Roe Crest Drive, North Mankato, Minnesota 56003
capstonepub.com

Copyright © 2025 by Capstone. All rights reserved. No part of this publication may
be reproduced in whole or in part, or stored in a retrieval system, or transmitted in any
form or by any means, electronic, mechanical, photocopying, recording, or otherwise,
without written permission of the publisher.

Library of Congress Cataloging-in-Publication Data is available on the Library of
Congress website.

ISBN: 9781669088387 (hardcover)
ISBN: 9781669088356 (paperback)
ISBN: 9781669088363 (ebook PDF)

Summary: Readers face the challenges of being lost in a snowstorm, inspired by the
experiences of real people.

Editorial Credits
Editor: Mandy Robbins; Designer: Dina Her; Media Researcher: Jo Miller;
Production Specialist: Tori Abraham

Image Credits:
Getty Images: Andrew Merry, 42, Evgeni Dinev Photography, 49, Jasmin Merdan,
62, Jasmin Merdan, 98, MICHELANGELOBOY, 36, Roberto Moiola/Sysaworld,
71, twildlife, 106; Shutterstock: Aastels, 4, AleksandarPhotograpy, 74, Burovtsev
Andrei, 31, Dmitry Naumov, 72, Evannovostro, 39, Good2, 25, Gorloff-KV, 10,
james_stone76, 80, Lonyks, 8, Melinda Nagy, 83, Mikadun, 6, mountainpix, 89,
Mumemories, cover, 1, Petair, 17, Tremens Productions, 57, zef art, 61

Design Elements:
Shutterstock: Here, Irina Gutyryak, Mariyana M, oxinoxi, railway fx, Stone36, Vik Y

Any additional websites and resources referenced in this book are not maintained,
authorized, or sponsored by Capstone. All product and company names are
trademarks™ or registered® trademarks of their respective holders.

Printed and bound in the USA. 6121

TABLE OF CONTENTS

INTRODUCTION
ABOUT YOUR ADVENTURE 5

CHAPTER 1
A DANGEROUS WINTER STORM 7

CHAPTER 2
WRONG TURNS. 11

CHAPTER 3
A SNOWY QUEST. .43

CHAPTER 4
LOST ON THE MOUNTAIN. 73

CHAPTER 5
SURVIVING A SNOWSTORM 99

TRUE STORIES OF SURVIVAL. 106
S.T.O.P. TO SURVIVE 108
OTHER PATHS TO EXPLORE 109
GLOSSARY. 110
READ MORE 111
INTERNET SITES 111
ABOUT THE AUTHOR 112

INTRODUCTION

ABOUT YOUR ADVENTURE

YOU are lost in a snowstorm. With few resources and no help, you're adrift in a sea of white. You can't see, and you're freezing. With the wind and snow pelting your face, every step is a struggle. YOU CHOOSE what path to take. Will you make it back to safety and warmth, or will the storm be your undoing?

Turn the page to begin your adventure.

CHAPTER 1

A DANGEROUS WINTER STORM

The day seems normal, like any other day. You have set off on an adventure. You are so focused on your mission that you barely pay attention to the weather. Then a few snowflakes fall from the sky. A few more fall, and the world looks like a pretty snow globe. But soon, the snowfall thickens. White flakes spin down until all you can see is white—white sky, white ground, white everywhere. You can barely see anything around you. You are in the middle of a major snowstorm.

Turn the page.

When the forecast warned of a winter storm, you should have stayed home. But you didn't listen. You set out and weren't prepared. Now you are stuck in a snowstorm, far from home. And worse, you are lost. Heavy, blowing snow impacts your vision. You can't see where you are going. Landmarks and signs are masked by high snowdrifts or blowing snow.

The cold and snow disorient you. Where are you? Are you going the right way? The winter weather is harsh and unforgiving. And when night falls, the elements will be even more dangerous. You know you need to find warmth and shelter soon.

You think back on your day and can't help wondering, "How did I end up here?"

- To have driven to a concert in a snowstorm, turn to page 11.
- To have gone on an errand for your grandma, turn to page 43.
- To have gone on a mountain hike with friends, turn to page 73.

CHAPTER 2

WRONG TURNS

It's the day you've been waiting for. Your favorite band is playing a concert in a nearby city, and you have tickets. Score!

Your friend Skyler arrives at your house as you are packing up the car. "You have everything we'll need?" he asks.

"Yep," you say. "I have money and the tickets. Hop in!"

Turn the page.

You both buckle into your car. You don't have a Bluetooth radio, so you start your playlist on your phone. Then you pull onto the highway toward the city.

Skyler sings along as you drive. When the playlist ends, he flips on the radio.

"Winter weather advisory," says the radio DJ. "A snowstorm is forecasted for the listening area."

Skyler looks at you nervously. You shrug.

"The sky looks clear to me!" you say.

"Yeah, keep going," he agrees. "We can't miss this concert!"

Then a few flakes begin to fall. Skyler checks his weather app.

"Looks like we're heading right into the storm," he says.

A few snowflakes won't keep you from the concert. "We've gone too far to turn back now," you say.

Soon, though, the flakes multiply into a whirling mass of white. Your knuckles are also white as you clutch the steering wheel. You slow your speed and quicken the windshield wipers. You can make out the taillights of the cars ahead of you, but just barely.

"Can you see okay to drive?" Skyler asks. His voice has a nervous pitch.

Turn the page.

"Yes," you say, trying to remain calm.

But the whirling snowflakes make you feel dizzy. Your windshield wipers are on the highest speed, but the snow is still blinding.

Brake lights flash, as the car ahead of you slows. Soon, traffic is almost at a standstill.

You glance at the clock. "We'll never make it to the concert in time," you groan.

Skyler pulls up a map on his phone. He waves toward an approaching exit.

"Maybe we should turn off here," he suggests. "We can take back roads to the city."

The road looks familiar, but you can't see enough of your surroundings to be sure.

- To take the exit, go to page 15.
- To keep going, turn to page 17.

You take the exit. Happy that the road is clear of cars, you pick up your speed. Small snow drifts have built up on the road, and your tires smash into them as you pass.

"We'll definitely make it now," you say. "How do we get to the city from here?"

Skyler looks down at his phone. "I don't know. The map isn't updating!"

You feel a little irritated but wave it off. You know you're going the right direction. You figure you'll make it to the city eventually.

But you don't see another car in sight. If this were another route to the city, certainly other cars would be on it too.

Turn the page.

"Is your map updating now?" you ask.

Skyler taps his phone. "No signal," he says.

He tries your phone too. Nothing.

"Let's just turn around," Skyler suggests.

"But then we're backtracking," you say. "We're already running late."

- To turn around, turn to page 21.
- To keep going, turn to page 24.

You stay on the highway, following the taillights in front of you. Most cars are moving slowly, but a few trucks fly past you. Their wheels spit snow onto your windshield.

After several miles, the traffic lessens. Soon, you feel as if you are the only car on the road.

"Where did everybody go?" you wonder aloud.

"I guess no one wants to be driving in this snowstorm," Skyler says.

Turn the page.

He looks at the clock. "We're not going to make it to the concert unless you pick up the pace," Skyler says.

He's right. The only reason you're out here in the snowstorm is to get to the concert. "Yeah, if we don't make it to the show, it's all for nothing," you agree.

You grip the steering wheel and step on the gas. A flurry of snow hits your windshield. The wipers bounce back and forth wildly, but not enough to clear your vision. You know you're going too fast for the conditions.

Panicked, you step on the brakes. Bad move. The car skids across the road, spins around, and nose-dives into the ditch. Your body flies forward into the locked seat belt. You hear a crunch as the car slams sideways into a post.

"Aaaah," moans Skyler. You are glad to hear his voice. But he doesn't sound so good.

"Are you okay?" you gasp.

"My arm!" he wails.

It's too dark to see much, but you can see the side of the car dented in, and Skyler's arm hanging loosely. It might be broken.

"I'll call 911," you say.

You feel around for your phone, but it must've flown out of the cup holder in the crash. You use voice commands to call 911. The call drops before you can give your location. You try again, but you can't get through. Skyler groans in pain.

"I'll see if there are any cars on the highway to flag down," you tell him. "I'll leave the car running so you don't freeze."

Turn the page.

You step out of the car and scramble up the bank toward the highway. The snow is blinding, and you don't see any headlights. After fifteen minutes, not a single vehicle has passed. You wonder if the highway department closed the road. You're covered in snow and freezing, and now darkness is starting to fall

Ahead, you can make out an overpass. Maybe you could find shelter there while you hope for a vehicle to come so you can flag it down. Or maybe you should go back to the car to wait it out with Skyler.

- To head to the overpass, turn to page 34.
- To go back to the car, turn to page 36.

Skyler is right. You don't know where you are. And if you keep going, you might get even more lost. It's best to turn around now.

You slow your speed, looking for a side road to pull into. But the ditches are pure white with snow. You can't see a thing.

"I'll have to do a U-turn," you tell Skyler.

As you aim toward the side of the road to swing a U-turn, the wheels catch in some snow. You rev the engine, but the wheels just spin.

"We're stuck," you groan.

"I'll get out and push," Skyler offers, reaching for the car door handle. He struggles to open the door against the powerful wind.

"Be careful!" you holler as he finally shoulders the door open.

Turn the page.

Your driver's education teacher taught you some tricks to get a car unstuck. Put the gear in low, and don't spin the tires. Just tap the gas lightly so the car rocks. You follow the steps as Skyler pushes.

But the tricks don't work. No matter how lightly you press the gas, the wheels spin, digging you deeper into the snowbank.

Skyler taps on the window, breathless, his hair speckled with snow. "Do you have a shovel?" he shouts. "Or some kitty litter?"

"Kitty litter?" you ask, confused.

Skyler sighs in frustration and gets back in the car. "Putting kitty litter under the wheels helps gain traction," he says. "We'll have to call someone."

You reach for your phone, but it doesn't light up. "It's dead!" you say. "We shouldn't have streamed all that music."

Skyler taps his phone. "I still can't get a signal anyway," he moans. "There's no service out here."

You dig around the car for a phone charger. But you must have forgotten to pack it.

"Someone will come along eventually," you say, trying to remain positive. "At least we have gas to keep the car running. We won't freeze!"

But an hour passes. The car is covered in snow. You're not sure anyone will see you even if they do pass by.

"Maybe one of us should go out and try to find help," Skyler suggests.

You aren't sure you should leave the car, but it may be the only way to get help.

- To go for help, turn to page 26.
- To stay in the car, turn to page 28.

"Let's keep going," you tell Skyler. "This road has to lead to the city. We're going the right direction."

You continue down the road, slowly and steadily. You don't want to drive too fast and slide into the ditch. Skyler fidgets with the radio.

"I can't get a station," he says. "We're in the middle of nowhere!"

You drive on, hoping you made the right choice. But you haven't. The road eventually turns to gravel. Then you come to a dead end. In front of you is a frozen lake, and across the lake you see streetlights. Finally, a town!

"We could turn back and try to find a way around the lake," Skyler suggests.

"But we could get stuck. Or more lost than we are now," you say. "What if we just drive across the lake. In this weather, it's bound to be frozen."

"That might work," he says.

- To drive across the lake, turn to page 38.
- To find a way around the lake, turn to page 40.

"Sitting around waiting isn't getting us anywhere," you say. "You stay here. I'll go out and try to find help."

You step out of the car into the bitter wind. The snow is up to your knees, and you trudge a few paces. It's hard to believe so much snow has fallen so quickly. You notice the car's muffler is jammed in a snowbank. That's not good. You don't want poisonous gas to back up into the cab and kill Skyler. You clear the vent and start walking.

You're already out of breath with the exertion and cold. Snow seeps into your shoes. The walk will be tough, but you're willing to try.

Wind whips around your head. You don't have a scarf or gloves. Tightening your hood around your head, you kick yourself for not being more prepared.

The road must lead somewhere, you think, so you walk along the edge. If a car comes, you can flag it down.

There's still enough daylight to see, but the falling snow obscures your view. You stomp through the snow, ignoring the bitter cold stiffening your toes.

Then you come to a small road that branches east. A dark patch of trees is clustered along the road. Maybe there's a house behind the trees. But you aren't sure you should veer off the main road.

- To take the side road, turn to page 29.
- To keep going on the main road, turn to page 31.

You think you read somewhere to stay in the vehicle in situations like this, so you do. Soon, you start to feel sleepy. Skyler has already drifted off in the passenger seat. You close your eyes and fall asleep too.

But you forgot one important piece of advice—to make sure to clear the snow from the tailpipe. The car fills with deadly carbon monoxide gas. You and Skyler never open your eyes again.

THE END

To follow another path, turn to page 9.

To learn more about survival in a snowstorm, turn to page 99.

The grove of trees is not far from the road. And it will be getting dark soon, and you won't be able to see a thing. You decide your best bet is to check out what's behind those trees.

The snow is high along the side road. Snowdrifts block your way. It doesn't look like anyone has driven down this road in a while. You begin to wonder if you've made a big mistake, but as you come to the grove of trees, you see a structure ahead.

Picking up your pace, you leap through the snow until you come to a small shed, nearly covered in snow. It looks abandoned, but it could still provide you with some shelter.

You know Skyler is waiting for you to return with help, but you are cold and windblown. You could rest in the shed for a while.

Turn the page.

You push on the door, and it flies open. You step inside, glad to be out of the wind and snow. Cold is seeping into your body, and you hop up and down to keep the blood flowing.

A sound above you catches your attention. *Creeeaak!* Before you can figure out what the noise is, the shed collapses under the weight of snow. You should have checked to make sure the building was sturdy before going inside. You are buried in snow and debris, never to emerge.

THE END

To follow another path, turn to page 9.
To learn more about survival in a snowstorm, turn to page 99.

You decide it's best to stick to the main road. Hopefully, a vehicle will come by, or you'll come upon a house.

The snow scuttles down, and daylight is fading. If you don't find help soon, you're afraid of what might happen.

Then you see headlights in the distance. The lights move slowly along the road toward you. You know you should never get in the car with a stranger, but you're hoping they'll have a phone to call for help. This could be a matter of life or death.

When the vehicle gets close, you jump up and down, waving your arms and yelling, "Stop!"

The car slows to a stop. To your relief, you see it's a state trooper. She rolls down her window. "You stranded?" she asks.

You nod and explain what happened, and she gestures you to get in. She says she'll pick up Skyler and then take you to the nearest town for help.

You warm your hands by the heat vents. "Why aren't you wearing gloves?" she demands. "You should always be prepared for a winter storm, especially when driving long distances!"

She's right. And now your fingers are burning. The tips are white with frostbite. You hope the damage isn't permanent, but at least you're alive.

When you reach your car, the trooper pulls over, lights flashing. Skyler jumps out of the car and rushes to the patrol car. "Get in!" you tell him.

"While you were gone, the car ran out of gas!" he explains breathlessly, sliding into the backseat. "I'm freezing."

The trooper shakes her head. "Always travel with a survival kit!" she says. "Include a blanket, jumper cables, a shovel, food, and a phone charger!"

You feel ashamed. But she's right. From now on, you'll be more prepared for any snowstorm that comes your way.

THE END

To follow another path, turn to page 9.
To learn more about survival in a snowstorm, turn to page 99.

You trudge toward the overpass. Through the snow, you can make out a shape. You're in luck. It's another car, parked under the overpass to wait out the storm.

You knock on the window, and the driver rolls it down.

"You stranded too?" he asks.

"We went off the road and hit a post," you tell him. "My friend is hurt!"

"I'll call for help!" the driver tells you.

Soon, you see the flashing lights of a rescue vehicle. Relieved, you point toward your car in the ditch.

Paramedics load Skyler into the ambulance, and you hop in too.

"We missed the concert," Skyler moans.

You nod. "I know, but at least we're safe."

As the ambulance makes its way to the emergency room, you vow to yourself to pay more attention to the forecast next time. Just because the sky is clear, doesn't mean a storm isn't looming.

THE END

To follow another path, turn to page 9.

To learn more about survival in a snowstorm, turn to page 99.

Since the highway is deserted, you don't think there's much hope for help out here. You might as well be warm with Skyler and wait out the storm. You trudge back toward the car.

But you don't see it. You fight through the snow, looking for tire tracks that show where you went off the road. But so much snow has fallen that the tracks are covered. You should have turned the hazard lights on before you left the vehicle.

The storm has really picked up. You are lost in a sea of white. You can no longer see the overpass, either.

"Skyler!" you holler but your voice is lost in the wind.

You wander until you collapse in the snow. As you drift into a sleep you will never wake from, you hope someone finds Skyler before it's too late for him too.

THE END

To follow another path, turn to page 9.

To learn more about survival in a snowstorm, turn to page 99.

"I don't want to get stuck or lost," you say. "We'd better just drive across."

You gun it and drive down the embankment to the frozen edge of the lake.

"Are you sure it's frozen all the way across?" Skyler asks, leaning forward to peer out the window.

You gesture to the whiteness all around you. "Of course! Look at it out there."

But as soon as you finish your sentence, you hear a crack. Uh-oh. You shift the car into reverse, but it's too late. The ice cracks around the car like a spiderweb. The car plunges into the icy depths, taking you and Skyler with it.

THE END

To follow another path, turn to page 9.
To learn more about survival in a snowstorm, turn to page 99.

"I don't think we should drive across," you tell Skyler. "Let's try to find a way around it."

Skyler agrees. You turn the car around, looking for a road that branches off. You take the first side road you see.

The snow is still falling, but the road is mostly clear, with only patches of snow. To your relief, the wind off the lake is blowing most of it off the road.

"Look!" Skyler points.

In the distance, you see a red and blue sign. It's a gas station! You hope it's open. You pull into the lot, and a station attendant peers out and waves.

"Civilization!" Skyler exclaims.

You go inside to buy supplies and ask directions to the nearest lodging. To your delight, the attendant offers to let you hunker down in the store until the storm has passed.

You are relieved. You don't want to drive any farther in the storm. It has been a day of bad decisions, but you're glad you made the right one this time. You've learned some valuable lessons about being prepared for bad weather, and you'll never be unprepared again.

THE END

To follow another path, turn to page 9.

To learn more about survival in a snowstorm, turn to page 99.

CHAPTER 3

A SNOWY QUEST

It's winter break, and you and your little sister, Sarya, are staying at your grandma's house for a week. Usually, you have a lot of fun there, but this time Grandma is sick. For the past few days, she's had a terrible cough, and now she can't even get out of bed.

Turn the page.

You scrounge through the bathroom cabinet for medicine to help her, but you find nothing. Your grandma just moved into a different house on the outskirts of town, and you've only been here once before. Maybe you're not looking in the right place. You and Sarya climb onto step stools and search all the bathroom and kitchen cupboards. No medicine. And not much food either.

As you search the cupboards, you hear Grandma coughing violently from her bedroom.

Sarya looks at you wide-eyed. "We have to help her!" she says.

"Let's go get some medicine," you say. "We can stop for groceries too."

"Shouldn't one of us stay here with her?" Sarya asks.

You think, then you shake your head. "I'll need you to help carry the bags," you say.

Tapping softly on your grandma's bedroom door, you call, "Grandma, we're going to get you some cough syrup and food. Be back soon!"

She doesn't answer. She might not have heard you. You scribble a note and leave it on the counter. When you and Sarya have bundled into your winter coat and boots, you head out.

"I don't think the market is very far," you say confidently as you head down the hill.

"I remember passing it on the way here!" Sarya agrees.

A brisk wind carries her voice away. You tighten your hood. A few snowflakes fall, landing on your cheeks and eyelashes.

Turn the page.

"Oooh, snow!" shrieks Sarya. She runs ahead and twirls under the flakes.

"Come on," you say. "Remember, we're on a mission!"

You continue down the sidewalk. The snow falls ever faster. The flakes are thick and furious. You have to keep wiping snow from your eyelashes to see.

"How much farther?" your sister asks.

You look around. The sudden snow has covered the streets. Nothing looks familiar.

You should check the internet for directions. You reach in your pocket for your phone.

"Oh no!" you exclaim. "My phone is in my other jacket."

You're a little worried about finding your way without a map, but the town isn't that big. You're confident the market is close.

"Let's keep going," you say. "The market can't be more than half a mile from Grandma's."

"I think we should turn left," Sarya says.

You look in the direction she's pointing, but nothing looks familiar that way either. And you don't know if you should turn off the main road.

- To follow your sister's direction, turn to page 48.
- To keep forging ahead, turn to page 50.

Even though you are doubtful, you turn in the direction Sarya pointed. If you don't find anything, you can turn back.

Sarya runs ahead, and you struggle through the snow after her. It is even more blinding on this road, and you realize there are no streetlights. And no houses, at least not nearby.

"Stay close!" you yell to Sarya and reach out to link arms with her. "The storm is getting worse. I guess we should have checked the forecast before we left."

With her free arm, Sarya points ahead. "Look!" she says.

Up ahead, you see a small structure. You were hoping it would be a house, but it's just a small shed.

"Maybe we should hang out here until the storm dies down?" Sarya suggests.

Maybe it's best to hunker down until the worst of the storm is over. But you want to keep trying to find civilization. Maybe you should turn back.

- To turn back, turn to page 52.
- To stay in the shed, turn to page 62.

"Let's keep going straight," you say. "This is the main road. I'm sure we'll find the market."

The wind slaps snow against your face as you trudge along. The whiteness of the snow blinds you. You hold tight to Sarya's hand, so you don't lose her.

Soon, you can no longer see any houses, just a path that keeps going through a thicket of trees.

"We're at the park!" Sarya says excitedly. She slips from your grasp and takes off running ahead of you.

The park is vaguely familiar, but you're totally turned around. You don't know how to get to the store from here. You're pretty sure you went the wrong way, and the weather is getting worse.

"Sarya!" you holler into the wind. "We have to turn back!"

When you catch up to her, she's standing at the edge of a frozen pond and pointing across.

"Look! There's a road on the other side," she says. "Let's take a shortcut across the pond."

If you turn around, you're only doubling back the way you came. Going across the pond might lead you to a market or somewhere you might find shelter. But you might have a better chance of making it to your grandma's if you turn back.

- To take a shortcut across the pond, turn to page 54.
- To turn back the way you came, turn to page 67.

"Let's turn back toward the streetlights," you say. There's nothing out here.

You turn back, struggling through the wind. Ahead, you see a house nestled in some trees.

"I know this house," you say. "I think this is where Grandma's friends live!"

"I hope they're home!" Sarya says.

But you are doubtful. The house looks dark. You knock loudly. No one answers.

"What do we do now?" Sarya asks. She is shivering, and you are both covered in snow. You hope she isn't getting hypothermia.

"We could keep going," you say. "Maybe there's another house around here."

Sarya shakes her head. "Or we could try to get in. Maybe through the windows?"

You aren't sure. You don't want to break in or trespass. But you are lost. And the wind and cold are dangerous.

"Listen," Sarya says. "Do you hear that?"

Through the roar of the storm, you hear another roar. The roar of an engine.

Sarya tugs on your arm. "Someone's out here!" she says. "Let's go toward the noise. Maybe we can flag them down!"

You hesitate. It's hard to see or move through the thick, blowing snow. But the house is locked. If you keep trying to get in, you might miss your chance to flag someone down. You need to save Sarya, and yourself.

- To try to get into the house, turn to page 56.
- To head toward the engine noise, turn to page 58.

You decide that a shortcut across the pond is the best option. Then you can reach the road on the other side of the park and possibly some sort of shelter.

"Let's go," you say, pointing to the pond.

You step out onto the pond and shuffle slowly along the ice. "Remember to waddle like a penguin on the ice!" you call.

But Sarya doesn't hear you. She launches herself onto the ice and breaks into a run. The ice is slippery, and she loses her balance, falling hard onto the frozen surface.

"My leg!" she wails. "I think it's broken!"

You shuffle as quickly as you can to her side, hoping she is just being dramatic. But her tears are real. Bending down to inspect her leg, you realize with dread that her leg is flopped to the side.

You help Sarya slide across the ice, but when you reach the other side of the pond, the snow is so deep that you know she won't be able to walk with her injured leg. You'll have to carry her.

Carrying Sarya is hard work. She's not as little as she used to be, and it's a struggle to keep your balance in the snow. Huffing and puffing, you pause and look around.

The white snow obscures your view, but you see a patch of trees ahead. You know it will be dark soon, so maybe you should take shelter in the trees. You're not sure how much farther you can carry her.

But Sarya shakes her head. "Please, we need to find help!" she says.

- To keep going, turn to page 60.
- To take shelter in the trees, turn to page 69.

"Okay, we can try to get in," you say.

Since the owners are friends of your grandma, you know they won't mind if you take shelter from the storm. Sarya smiles, relieved. You realize just how cold and scared she is.

You try the door, but it's locked. "Let's go around back!" you say, and trudge through the deep snow to the back.

The door to the attached garage is unlocked, and you get inside the house. You were hoping for a nice warm house, but the air inside is cold. The thermostat is in the kitchen, and when you raise the temperature, the heat doesn't kick in.

"It's broken," you sigh. You try to switch on the lights, but they don't work either. The power is out.

"There's a fireplace in the living room," Sarya says, pointing. "But there's no firewood."

"I'll go out and find some," you tell her.

"No!" she says. "Don't go back out in the storm!"

You don't want to freeze in here. Besides, you won't go far. But maybe Sarya is right. You don't really want to go back out there either.

- To go out and find firewood, turn to page 64.
- To stay in the house, turn to page 65.

You and Sarya head toward the noise you heard. But you see and hear nothing but the sound of the wind. Whoever it was is long gone now.

But maybe you'll find another house out here, with someone home. You keep going until you come to a hill. The snow is deeper now too.

"Walk in my footsteps," you tell Sarya.

The snow bats your face, and you are breathless. "Just a little longer. We're almost to the top," you call back to her.

But she doesn't answer. You whirl around. She isn't there. You've lost her.

You run back down the hill, calling her name. Then you stumble over a mound and go flying face-first into the snow.

The mound moves and stands up. It's Sarya.

"I fell!" she cries. "And you were too far ahead to hear me!"

"You should've stayed closer to me!" you say. You are angry, but not at her. You should've made sure you didn't lose each other.

"I have an idea," you say. You pull off your belt and weave it through her belt loop and yours. Now you won't lose her.

When you reach the top of the hill, all you see is more white. No houses. No lights.

"Maybe we should build a snow shelter," Sarya says.

You agree. You need to get out of the elements.

Turn to page 70.

You keep trudging, letting Sarya down every once in a while to catch your breath. Your back and shoulders ache. But you won't give up. You have to save Sarya, and yourself.

Through the roar of the wind, you think you hear an engine. You stop and listen, but whatever it was is gone. It must have been your imagination. So you trudge on through the snow.

The park is larger than you imagined. Or maybe you are just going in circles.

"We have to stop," you holler over your shoulder to Sarya.

She doesn't answer. Maybe she has passed out from the pain. Or maybe she has hypothermia. You know you have to get out of the elements. Building a shelter is your only hope.

You reach a small hill and set Sarya down. She is awake now, but she can barely hold her head up and keeps mumbling.

Turn to page 69.

The shed is cold, but it's better than being out in the snowstorm. You're shivering. You want to just curl up and sleep on the floor of the shed, but you know it's best to keep moving.

"Show me your best dance moves," you say.

Sarya breaks into a dance, and you do too. When you're tired of dancing, you march in place. Even though you are still in danger, you are having fun.

When you no longer hear the howl of the wind, you poke your head outside. The storm isn't over, but the flakes have slowed. And you can see streetlights shining ahead.

"Let's go," you holler to Sarya.

As you trudge through the snow, you see a sign up ahead. It's the market! Sarya was right all along.

You survived the snowstorm, and now you'll even manage to bring some food and medicine to your grandma.

THE END

To follow another path, turn to page 9.
To learn more about survival in a snowstorm, turn to page 99.

You step outside into the blustery wind. You head toward the backyard, hoping to find some fallen branches. Ahead, you see a fallen tree. The storm must have knocked it over. You can pull off the smaller branches to use as kindling.

As you get closer, you see that the tree has hit a power line. Wires dangle across the branches. This must be why the power is out. You assume the lines are dead. You reach for one of the branches and feel a zap! A shock of electricity sizzles through your body. Too late, you realize you stepped on a wire. And it was not dead.

You jump back, but you land on another live wire. As you fall backward, electrocuted, your only thought is that at least Sarya is safe inside. You hope the owners come home soon.

THE END

To follow another path, turn to page 9.

To learn more about survival in a snowstorm, turn to page 99.

64

"Okay, I won't go out," you tell her. "But how will we stay warm?"

"I know!" she says. She runs down the hall and comes back with an armload of towels. "Grab the blankets from the couch," she says.

You bring blankets back into the kitchen, and she shuts all the doors to the kitchen and stuffs towels underneath the doors. "This will help keep the heat in," she tells you.

You both huddle underneath the blankets. Then you notice that the stove is gas. "I bet it'll work, even without electricity," you say. "We could light the oven and warm up the room!"

"That's a bad idea," she tells you. "It could release gas, like . . ."

"Carbon monoxide," you finish. "Yeah, bad idea."

Turn the page.

So you stay huddled together. Once in a while, you stand and do jumping jacks to get your blood flowing.

In the morning, you wake and look outside. The snow has stopped. Cars are moving along the road. Now it will be easier to find someone to help you.

You wake Sarya. "We survived," you say. "Now let's get back to Grandma!"

THE END

To follow another path, turn to page 9.

To learn more about survival in a snowstorm, turn to page 99.

You turn back the way you came. But the snow is pelting your face and drifting into deep piles around your feet. Ahead, you see a grove of trees.

"We should take shelter for a while," you say.

"Okay," Sarya agrees.

You reach the grove of trees. You hoped the trees would provide some shelter from the wind, but gusts still hurtle full force into your body.

"Maybe we could make some kind of windbreak," Sarya says.

It's a good idea. As quickly as you can, you snap branches off the trees and stack them together against the trees, packing snow along with the branches. The windbreak helps fend off the wind and the blowing snow, at least for now. You and Sarya huddle together, shivering.

Turn the page.

Then, you hear the rumble of a motor and some shouting. When you stand up, you see two snowmobilers coming your way. You jump and wave to catch their attention. The snowmobilers roar toward you. They are wearing uniforms, and as they get closer, you see they are park rangers.

"The storm kicked up fast," one of the rangers says. "We wanted to make sure no one was lost out here in the snow."

The other ranger nods at your makeshift windbreak. "Nice work there," she says.

After you explain what happened, the rangers offer to take you to the market and then to your grandma's. You and Sarya hop on the back of the snowmobiles, safe and about to be warm again.

THE END

To follow another path, turn to page 9.

To learn more about survival in a snowstorm, turn to page 99.

"I can't carry you any farther," you tell Sarya. "Let's just take a break here so I can catch my breath. The trees will shelter us."

At first, the trees provide shelter from the snow. You and Sarya huddle together, watching the storm come down around you in heavy, wet flakes.

A sudden gust of wind shakes the trees above you. The branches, overloaded with heavy snow, creak under the pressure. One branch falls and then another. One knocks you on the head, and your head spins. As everything goes black, your last thought is of Sarya. With her broken leg, she won't be able to dodge any falling branches or go to find help. You hope someone finds her, soon.

THE END

To follow another path, turn to page 9.

To learn more about survival in a snowstorm, turn to page 99.

You work quickly to build a snow cave on the side of the hill. First, you dig an entrance tunnel, then carve out a raised interior. You don't want to suffocate, so you dig out small ventilation holes so you can breathe. You make the cave big enough for both of you.

When the cave is done, you and Sarya crawl inside. Then she hands you her bright pink belt from her coat, and you stick it on top of the cave.

"Maybe this will help someone find us," she mumbles.

She's right. You hunker down, huddling together. You realize the snow cave is so much warmer than being out in the wind. Eventually, you hear shouts. You crawl out of the cave to find two park rangers heading toward you on snowmobiles. You realize the snowmobiles must be the engines you heard earlier.

"We're looking for anyone who's lost in this storm," they tell you. "And we spotted the pink belt."

"That was my sister's idea," you say. "And I built the cave."

As the rangers help you and Sarya through the snow to their snowmobiles, they commend you for your quick thinking to survive being lost in the snowstorm.

THE END

To follow another path, turn to page 9.
To learn more about survival in a snowstorm, turn to page 99.

CHAPTER 4

LOST ON THE MOUNTAIN

At last, the day has arrived—your hiking trip to a nearby mountain. It's a crisp day in late October, and you are excited to see the fall colors from the top of the mountain. You pack your gear—water, protein bars, a knife, and a compass. You leave your headlamp at home. It's just a day hike, after all.

You meet up with your friends, Tasha, Rob, José, and Kaylee. You aren't a very experienced hiker, but you are excited for the opportunity to hike with your friends.

Turn the page.

You all head up the mountain trail, the sun shining through wispy clouds. But as the hike goes on, heavy clouds rush in. Snow begins whirling around you. When you checked the forecast before your trip, there was only a 30 percent chance of snow.

"Here's our 30 percent," Kaylee says, rolling her eyes.

"I thought we were in the clear," you say. You pull out your phone to check your weather app, but there's no cell service. No one else has a signal either.

"I'm sure it'll pass," Rob says. "It's only October!"

"I don't know," says Tasha, her face to the sky. "It's getting worse!"

"Maybe we should turn back," says José. Tasha nods in agreement.

"No way," says Kaylee. "I'm heading to the summit."

"Same," says Rob.

They all turn to look at you. "Well?" they ask. "What are you going to do?"

- To keep going to the summit with Rob and Kaylee, turn to page 76.
- To go back down with José and Tasha, turn to page 78.

"I'm going up to the summit," you say confidently. "It's the reason I came!"

"And there will probably be cell service at the top," Rob agrees.

The three of you hike up the mountain. Rob leads the way. A marathon runner, he is quick and agile. The snow keeps falling. It slashes against your face and makes your eyes water.

Soon, you can barely see anything. It's total whiteout conditions. You realize it won't matter if you make the summit. You won't be able to see the view anyway.

Rob stops abruptly ahead of you. "Shoot!" he says. "I can't see the trail anymore."

"Let's go around the south side of the mountain," Kaylee says. "Since the wind is coming from the north, the storm shouldn't be as bad there."

You nod in agreement. Kaylee has had a lot of experience sailing with her family. Because of it, she knows how to read the weather, even in winter.

Rob shakes his head. "I think the trail goes straight ahead. We should try to stick to it."

Kaylee crosses her arms, throwing an irritated look at Rob.

"What do you think?" Kaylee asks.

You pause, considering the options. You like Kaylee's idea of heading to the south side of the mountain. But maybe you should stick to the trail, like Rob suggested.

- To stick to the trail, turn to page 82.
- To head to the southern side of the mountain, turn to page 87.

You really wanted to make it to the summit, but with this weather, the best decision is to hike back down with José and Tasha. You trust them. José is an experienced hiker, and Tasha has taken survivalist classes.

At first, you follow the trail. The snow is falling faster now, and you place your hands on each other's shoulders to stay together.

José comes to an abrupt stop. "Where are we?" he asks.

You and Tasha look around. Nothing looks familiar. You've lost the trail.

"We're lost," Tasha says.

"Stay here," José says. "I'll see what's ahead." With José's hiking experience, he will be good at scouting out a route. He disappears into a whirl of snow.

You wait. Five minutes pass. José doesn't return.

"Should we go after him?" Tasha asks.

You nod. "Yes. But we need to stay together."

You follow the faint outlines of José's footprints. Then you hear someone shout, "Help!" It's José.

You follow the footprints to the edge of a crevasse. José has fallen in. He's clutching his leg and moaning. When he sees you, he gives a half-hearted wave.

"What do we do?" Tasha asks. "Our phones don't work out here."

"We have to try to save him," you say. "Hold my leg. I'll scuttle to the edge and see if he can grasp my arm."

Turn the page.

You lie down on your stomach and inch your way to the edge of the crevasse, with Tasha holding tightly to your leg. José tries to reach your hand, but the crevasse is too deep. And José is too injured to stand up.

"Hand me your scarf," you tell Tasha.

She unwinds her bright orange scarf and gives it to you. Then you lean over the edge again, dangling the scarf.

But José still can't reach it.

"We'll go get help!" Tasha calls down to him.

"How?" you mutter. "We're lost. And we shouldn't leave him."

"You stay here," Tasha says. "I'll go."

"Leave me!" José calls. "It's no use for us all to be stuck out here! Get to safety."

"I could leave my scarf here to mark where José is," Tasha adds.

You don't want Tasha to go on her own. But you also don't want to leave José.

- To go with Tasha to find help, turn to page 85.
- To stay with José, turn to page 92.

81

"I think the trail is the best option," you say. "We don't know what lies south."

Reluctantly, Kaylee agrees, and the three of you trek up the trail, or at least what you think is the trail. Suddenly, Rob shouts in joy, pointing ahead to a plaque among the rocks. You've reached the summit!

The three of you clink your water bottles together in celebration. As you tip up the bottle to take a sip, you realize it's empty. You should have made more of an effort to conserve your water. But at least there is snow all around you. And snow is just frozen water, right?

As you head back down the trail, the wind pummels you. The storm has gotten worse.

When you come to a grouping of boulders, Rob stops. "These boulders are too slippery to climb down."

"We could move sideways across the mountain until we find a safer route down," Rob suggests.

"Or we could go back up and try to find a different way down," Kaylee says.

They both look at you to chime in. What do you think?

- To move sideways across the mountain, turn to page 84.
- To go back up and find a different way down, turn to page 90.

83

You move along the side of the mountain. The terrain is rough, and there's no safe path down. The wind blasts so hard against your face that your cheeks flap.

"Let's try going down here!" Rob yells, pointing to a break in the trees. Though the snow is covering the slope, it looks slick and rocky.

"Maybe we should keep going sideways," Kaylee suggests.

You are unsure. The sooner you start trekking down the mountain, the sooner you will find safety. But you could get hurt on the rocky terrain.

- To head down the mountain, turn to page 95.
- To keep going sideways, turn to page 97.

"We need to find help," you tell Tasha. "Or José might not make it."

Tasha pulls out her compass. "This way," she points.

You make your way slowly, the wind battering you. Tasha leads the way, taking out her compass often to check.

You come to a grove of trees. "This looks familiar," you say.

Tasha looks around. "That's because we just went in a circle!" she says.

"How did that happen?" you gasp. "We were using the compass to guide us!"

Tasha sighs angrily. "Sometimes, iron deposits in the environment can throw off the magnets in a compass," she says.

Turn the page.

"I wish I had studied the map more closely," she adds.

"It's not your fault," you say. "Anyone can get lost in a snowstorm."

Just then, you hear a rumble.

"What's that sound?" you ask.

"Avalanche!" Tasha yells and begins to run.

As the snow barrels toward you, Tasha shouts, "Roll with the snow!"

But it is too late. The avalanche knocks you off your feet and buries you. You and your friends' adventure has come to a tragic end.

THE END

To follow another path, turn to page 9.
To learn more about survival in a snowstorm, turn to page 99.

"Let's go south," you say. "Even if there's no trail, with better weather, we might be able to find our way."

Kaylee takes the lead, Rob follows, and you bring up the rear. The wind bats your face. You slow your speed so you can catch your breath. You are trudging along, far behind, when suddenly, you trip and fall to your knees. You realize one of your bootlaces came untied, and you tripped over it. How embarrassing! You should have made sure your laces were tight.

Quickly, you tie your laces and jump to your feet. But now you can no longer see your friends.

"Kaylee? Rob?" you call into the wind. No answer. They must have thought you were right behind them. But now you are lost on the mountain, alone in a snowstorm.

Turn the page.

Then you see something down the slope. It could be Kaylee and Rob, or maybe the others in your group. You need to get down to them, and quickly.

You remember a technique you read about called glissading. Glissading is a way of sliding down a mountain without skis. It can be dangerous, but you're desperate. You break off a nearby branch to help propel you. Then you bend your knees and push off.

At first, the glissade is fun. You slide quickly down the slope. But then you lose your balance and topple over, tumbling wildly down the side of the mountain. When you finally come to a stop, you are amazed you are still alive. But when you try to stand, you can't. Both ankles are in pain. They may be broken.

You will never catch up with your friends now. You should have called to Rob and Kaylee to let them know you were falling behind. Now you are alone with two broken ankles. It will take a miracle to save you.

THE END

To follow another path, turn to page 9.
To learn more about survival in a snowstorm, turn to page 99.

You trek back up the mountain. The snow has obscured the sun, and none of you realize how quickly nightfall is coming. In just a few minutes, the sky has gone from whitish yellow to a dull gray.

"We're going to have to hunker down for the night," Kaylee says.

"Yeah, we can't hike back down in the dark," you agree.

"Luckily, I have this!" Rob opens his pack and pulls out an emergency mylar blanket. "I use these to keep warm after marathons."

"Now we just need to find a good place to stay," Kaylee says.

You remember passing an overhanging lip on the way up. "I think there's a spot right over here," you say. Your friends follow you to the overhang.

"Great spot!" Kaylee says.

"This will provide some shelter from the wind," Rob agrees.

The three of you huddle under the blanket, nibbling on protein bars. You scoop snow into your water bottles and melt it with your body heat so you can drink it. You weren't prepared for a winter storm, but at least you have some survival skills and supplies.

When the sun comes up, the snowstorm has passed. You head down the mountain. The three of you are relieved to have made it to safety. This is a climb you will never forget.

THE END

To follow another path, turn to page 9.

To learn more about survival in a snowstorm, turn to page 99.

"I'm going to stay with José," you tell Tasha.

She nods. "Then I'll stay too. We have a better chance of survival if we stick together."

Although José is in pain, he is grateful for your company.

"I wonder how long this storm will last," you say.

Tasha looks up at the sky. "Higher elevations are colder and have more snow," she says. "It might not even be snowing anymore at the base of the mountain."

"Since we don't know when it will stop snowing, we should build a shelter," Tasha says. "The snow is deep enough here that we can build a trench. A trench will help block the wind."

You and Tasha start digging. "The trench should be at least three feet deep," Tasha tells you. "And wide enough for both of us."

As you dig, you call down to José every once in a while, to make sure he's okay. You are glad the crevasse is keeping him sheltered from the violent wind and pelting snow.

When the trench has been carved out, Tasha places her hiking poles across the top. She digs a mylar emergency blanket from her pack and lays it over the poles. "Now we cover it with snow for insulation," she says.

When the trench is finished, you and Tasha slide in. At first, it's cold, but your body heat keeps you both warm, and the trench shelters you from the wind.

Turn the page.

In the morning, you hear the sounds of a helicopter. "They're looking for us!" Tasha says. She slithers out of the trench and waves her bright orange scarf.

The helicopter touches down, and rescue workers rush out. You point to the crevasse.

"Our friend is down there!" you exclaim.

The rescuers pull José from the crevasse. You are all safe and alive, happy to survive getting lost in a snowstorm. Your thoughts turn to your two friends who attempted the summit. You hope they are okay too.

THE END

To follow another path, turn to page 9.
To learn more about survival in a snowstorm, turn to page 99.

You need to get to safety as soon as possible. "Let's go down," you say.

Rob goes first. He sits down and slides forward using his feet. Toward the bottom, he stands and jumps. Kaylee follows, jumping at the bottom too. Then you go. As you slide, Rob shouts something at you. But you can't hear him.

Splash! You land in a rushing creek.

"I tried warning you!" Rob says.

"That's why we both jumped at the bottom," Kaylee adds.

Rob reaches out a hand to help you to your feet. You are soaked up to your knees.

"Take off your socks," Kaylee tells you. "Wet clothing will increase your chances of hypothermia and frostbite."

Turn the page.

You peel off your socks and stuff them under your shirt. Kaylee uses her sleeve to dry out the inside of your boots as much as possible. Then you continue on. Soon, everything around you begins to look familiar.

"Look! The trail!" Rob shouts.

You look in the direction he's pointing and see a yellow spike that marks the trail. He's right.

The three of you make your way down the trail. Tasha and José are waiting in the car.

"We were worried about you!" Tasha says.

Your wet feet are cold, and you are limping, but Kaylee's advice to take off your socks saved you from a worse fate.

THE END

To follow another path, turn to page 9.
To learn more about survival in a snowstorm, turn to page 99.

You keep trudging forward. You are cold and so thirsty. You know you need to hydrate. You pause and scoop some snow into your mouth. Then another scoop and another.

Kaylee looks back at you. "Stop that!" she orders. "You need to melt the snow to drink it!"

Suddenly, you start to feel worse. The snow has made your body temperature drop. You feel delirious and confused. Hypothermia sets in.

"Keep moving," Rob commands.

But you can't. You collapse. They try to rouse you, but it's no use. They try to carry you, but the terrain is too dangerous. Heartbroken, they leave you in your final resting place.

THE END

To follow another path, turn to page 9.

To learn more about survival in a snowstorm, turn to page 99.

CHAPTER 5

SURVIVING A SNOWSTORM

A winter weather event, such as a snowstorm, can be hazardous and even deadly. Heavy or blowing snow can be blinding. Car accidents can happen. People can find themselves stranded on roads, unable to find shelter. Frigid temperatures may lead to frostbite and hypothermia. Power outages can expose people to cold temperatures indoors too. Winter storms can block roadways, making it impossible for rescue vehicles to get to those stranded or in need of medical care.

A snowstorm happens when more than 2 inches (5 centimeters) of snow falls at a time. A snowstorm becomes a blizzard when the storm is accompanied by high winds. When wind speeds are above 35 miles (56 kilometers) per hour and last at least three hours, the storm is classified as a blizzard. Blizzards create blowing snow conditions, making it difficult for people to see their surroundings. Blizzards also cause snowdrifts that can cover roads. Driving in a blizzard is dangerous because of loss of visibility and snowy road conditions.

Winter storms can often be predicted. Meteorologists use satellites, Doppler radars, and computer models to predict when and where a snowstorm will happen. They can also calculate the possible path of the storm.

When a winter storm is forecasted in your area, listen to local weather updates. The National Weather Service issues weather alerts for areas that should prepare for winter storms. There are three types of winter weather alerts.

- Winter Weather Watch: A Winter Weather Watch means that there is a possibility of winter weather in your area. You should be prepared for the likelihood of a winter storm.

- Winter Weather Advisory: A Winter Weather Advisory means that winter weather conditions are expected but may not be severe.

- Winter Weather Warning: A Winter Weather Warning means that a storm will impact your area, and you should be prepared. Heavy snow, strong winds, and freezing temperatures will make travel and being outdoors dangerous.

If a winter storm is headed your way, your best chance of survival is to stay home. Make sure you have water, nonperishable food, a flashlight, extra batteries, a candle, and a fully charged cell phone. If the power goes out, have your family stay in one room and close the door. This will keep the warmth inside. Wear layers.

When traveling during the winter, have a fully stocked safety kit in your car. Some items to include are a blanket, protein bars, a shovel, sand or cat litter, an ice scraper, a flashlight, bottled water, a candle and matches, and a cell phone charger.

Dress in several layers of loose-fitting, lightweight clothing. Layering clothing allows you to avoid sweating and then getting chilled. Make sure you have a hat, scarf, and gloves or mittens.

If your vehicle gets stuck in snow, make sure conditions are safe enough to get out and shovel. If this doesn't work, call for roadside assistance.

When stranded, stay inside your vehicle. Run the motor for 10 minutes every hour for heat. Be sure to clear snow away from the exhaust pipe. This keeps carbon monoxide from entering the car. Crack a window for fresh air if possible. Do not leave the vehicle to walk for help, as you could become lost or disoriented.

If you are caught outside in a snowstorm, try to find shelter. Stay with your group and don't send anyone out alone.

If sheltering in a shed or other structure, make sure the structure is sturdy and won't collapse under the weight of snow.

If there is no structure around, find an overhang or trees to block the wind. Another option is to build a snow cave. Make sure the cave has an opening for air. Stay hydrated, but don't eat snow. Melt the snow before drinking it.

Making good decisions in a snowstorm is key. Stay calm and consider your options. By making the right choices, you can survive being lost in a snowstorm.

TRUE STORIES OF SURVIVAL

LAUREN WEINBERG

In 2011, college student Lauren Weinberg was driving toward Arizona's Mogollon Rim when her car became stuck in the snow. The area was remote, there was no one around for miles, and her cell phone was dead. Another snowstorm dropped more than two feet of snow around her. She stayed in her car for 10 days. She survived on two candy bars. She also melted snow in a bottle on her vehicle to drink.

TOMMY HENDRICKS AND MATT SMITH

In November 2016, Tommy Hendricks and Matt Smith hiked Mount of the Holy Cross in Colorado. On their way to the summit, a snowstorm hit. They pushed on to the summit, but it was too dark to hike back down. The boys spent the night under an overhanging of rock. In the morning, the storm had passed. They began descending the mountain but realized the trail was on the other side of the mountain. They tried to find their way using a compass. But iron deposits in the mountain threw off the magnets in their compass, so they kept ending up back where they started. They spent a second night out in the cold, but the next day, a helicopter rescued them.

SCHOOLCHILDREN'S BLIZZARD

In January 1888, a blizzard struck on the Dakotas and parts of Minnesota and Nebraska. The day had been mild, but cold air from Canada moved in quickly. The sudden afternoon storm caught people off guard. The blizzard killed 235 people, many of them children who were walking home from school. Some survived, though. After the wind tore the roof of a school off, teacher Minnie Freeman led 13 children to shelter almost a mile away. One man named William Kampen found shelter in a barn, huddling with pigs to stay warm.

S.T.O.P. TO SURVIVE

The best way to remember what to do if you find yourself in an emergency situation is to S.T.O.P. Each letter stands for an instruction you can follow to help get yourself to safety.

S.T.O.P.: Stop, Think, Observe, Plan

Stop: Stay calm and take in the situation.

Think: What do you need to do to survive? What supplies do you have on hand that you could use?

Observe: Look around. Do you see familiar landmarks? Can you tell what direction you're pointed?

Plan: Make a plan of action and never give up.

OTHER PATHS TO EXPLORE

1. In Chapter 2, you leave home without a winter survival kit. Imagine you had to leave home in bad weather. What items would you pack in a winter survival kit? How would you have used those items if your car broke down?

2. In Chapter 3, you build a snow cave to keep you and your sister out of the elements. What other types of shelters can you think of building? How would you keep yourself safe while drawing attention from rescue crews?

3. In Chapter 4, you are on a hike when a winter storm hits. You weren't prepared to hike in the snow. If you were to go on a winter hike, what gear might you wear? What might you bring in your pack? How would you use the gear in an emergency?

GLOSSARY

carbon monoxide (KAHR-buhn muh-NAHK-syd)—a colorless, odorless, and very poisonous gas formed by the incomplete burning of carbon

debris (duh-BREE)—the remains of something broken down or destroyed

elevation (e-luh-VAY-shuhn)—the height above the level of the sea

frostbite (FRAWST-byt)—the freezing of a surface or deeper layer of tissues of some part of the body

glissade (glih-SAHD)—to slide in a standing or squatting position down a snow-covered slope without the aid of skis

hypothermia (hy-po-THER-me-uh)—reduction of body temperature to a dangerously low level

meteorologist (mee-tee-ur-AWL-uh-jist)—a scientist who studies atmosphere, weather, and weather forecasting

summit (SUHM-it)—the highest point of a mountain

survivalist (surh-VYV-uh-list)—a person who practices how to survive in extreme conditions

READ MORE

Abramson, Marcia. *Extreme Cold and Blizzards.* Minneapolis: Bearport Publishing Company, 2024.

Clendenan Megan. *Life or Death on a Mountain: An Interactive Survival Adventure.* North Mankato, MN: Capstone, 2025.

Hayes, Vicki C. *Surviving a Blizzard.* Minnetonka, MN: Kaleidoscope, 2020.

INTERNET SITES

Blizzard
kids.britannica.com/kids/article/blizzard/476228

Blizzards
kids.nationalgeographic.com/science/article/blizzards

Winter Storm Safety
redcross.org/get-help/how-to-prepare-for-emergencies/
types-of-emergencies/winter-storm.html

ABOUT THE AUTHOR

Jessica Gunderson grew up in the small town of Washburn, North Dakota. She has a bachelor's degree from the University of North Dakota and an MFA in creative writing from Minnesota State University, Mankato. She has written more than 100 books for young readers. Her book *President Lincoln's Killer and the America He Left Behind* won a 2018 Eureka! Nonfiction Children's Book Silver Award. She currently lives in Madison, Wisconsin.